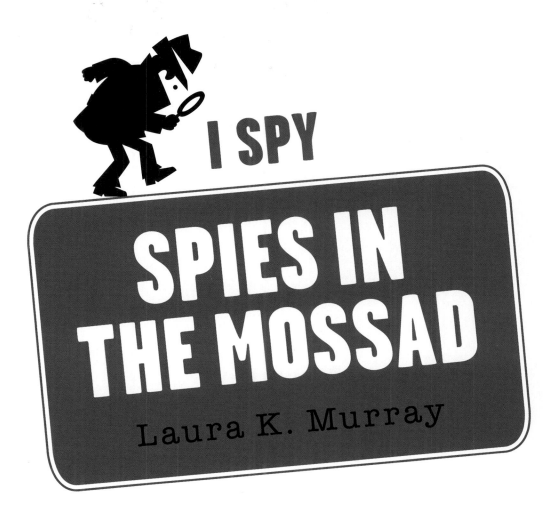

I SPY

SPIES IN THE MOSSAD

Laura K. Murray

Creative Education ✦ Creative Paperbacks

Published by Creative Education and Creative Paperbacks
P.O. Box 227, Mankato, Minnesota 56002
Creative Education and Creative Paperbacks
are imprints of **The Creative Company**
www.thecreativecompany.us

Design and production by **Christine Vanderbeek**
Art direction by **Rita Marshall**
Printed in the **United States of America**

Photographs by Alamy (CoverSpot, Heritage Image
Partnership Ltd, numb), Corbis (NIR ELIAS/Reuters,
Charles & Josette Lenars, Jeffrey L. Rotman), Getty Images
(Uriel Sinai/Stringer, GALI TIBBON/Stringer), Shutterstock
(Alexandr III, BeRad, Milos Djapovic, Globe Turner, M.
Luevanos, SoRad, tele52)

Library of Congress Cataloging-in-Publication Data
Murray, Laura K.
Spies in the Mossad / Laura K. Murray.
p. cm. — (I spy)
Includes index.
Summary: An early reader's guide to Mossad spies, intro-
ducing Israeli espionage history, famous agents such as
Cheryl Bentov, skills such as tailing, and the dangers all
spies face.

ISBN 978-1-60818-618-1 (hardcover)
ISBN 978-1-62832-230-9 (pbk)
ISBN 978-1-56660-665-3 (eBook)
1. Israel. Mosad le-modi'in ve-tafkidim meyuhadim—
Juvenile literature. 2. Spies—Israel—Juvenile literature.
3. Intelligence service—Israel—Juvenile literature. I. Title.

UB271.I8M87 2016
327.125694—dc23   2014048720

CCSS: RI.1.1, 2, 3, 4, 5, 6, 7, 10; RI.2.1, 2, 3, 5, 6, 7; RI.3.1,
3, 5, 7; RF.1.1, 3, 4; RF.2.4

First Edition HC 9 8 7 6 5 4 3 2 1
First Edition PBK 9 8 7 6 5 4 3 2 1

TABLE OF CONTENTS

I SPY

Israel became a
country in 1948.

Israel

SPIES WORK ALL OVER THE

world. They work in secret to
gather information. In Israel, spies
work for the Mossad. This group
began in 1949.

ISRAEL HAS HAD SPIES FOR

a long time. Hannah Senesh jumped out of a plane to rescue a group of Jews in 1944. Later, Israel's spies helped catch a **Nazi** (*NOT-zee*).

HELPING JEWS

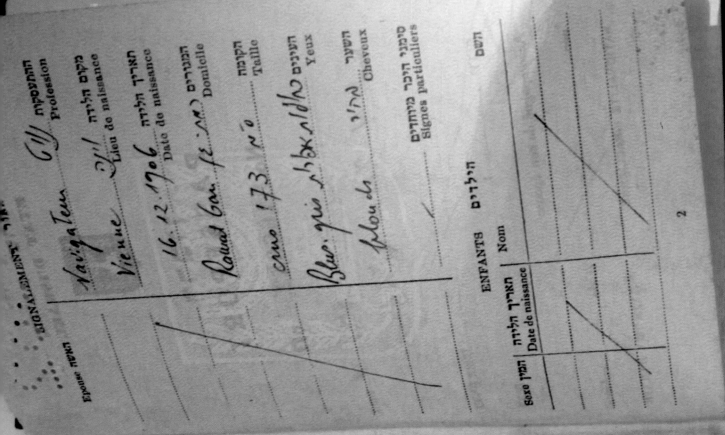

SIGNALEMENT

Hebrew	French	Value
	Profession	Navigateur (?)
	Lieu de naissance	Vienne
	Date de naissance	16.12.1906
	Domicile	Ramat Gan ...
	Taille	1 m 73
	Yeux	Bleu, gris ...
	Cheveux	blonds
	Signes particuliers	

Épouse

ENFANTS — Nom

Sexe	Date de naissance

2

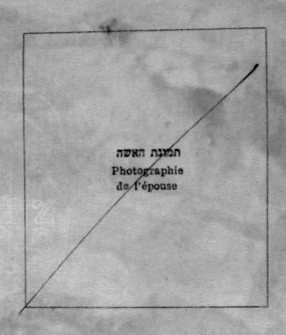

תמונת האשה
Photographie
de l'épouse

_____

Signature de l'épouse   חתימת האשה

3

Mossad spies traveled with fake passports.

ACTING AND TRAINING

ISRAELI SPIES MUST BE

good actors. They often work undercover. Spies use fake names. They stay hidden that way. Spy jobs can last for years!

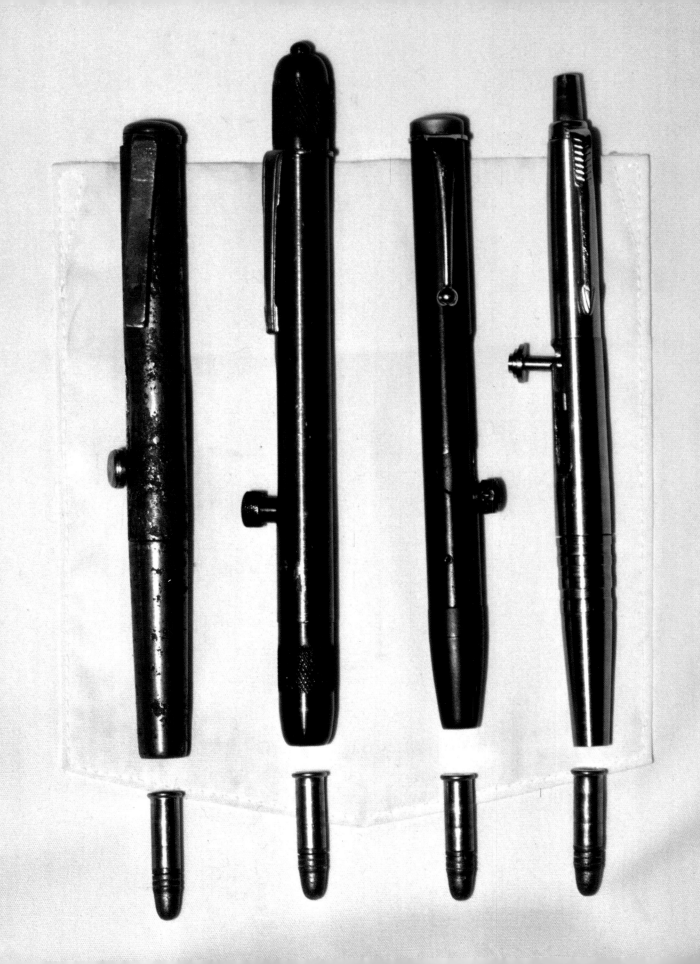

Bullet pens could be used as weapons.

THE MOSSAD TRAINING SCHOOL

is near Tel Aviv (*TELL ah-VEEV*). Agents spend about two years there. They learn how to lose a tail. They learn how to use weapons and break into rooms, too.

13

The Mossad keeps
some prisoners
near Tel Aviv.

CHERYL BENTOV WAS A

famous Mossad spy. She tricked

a man into trusting her. Then he

was kidnapped and put in jail.

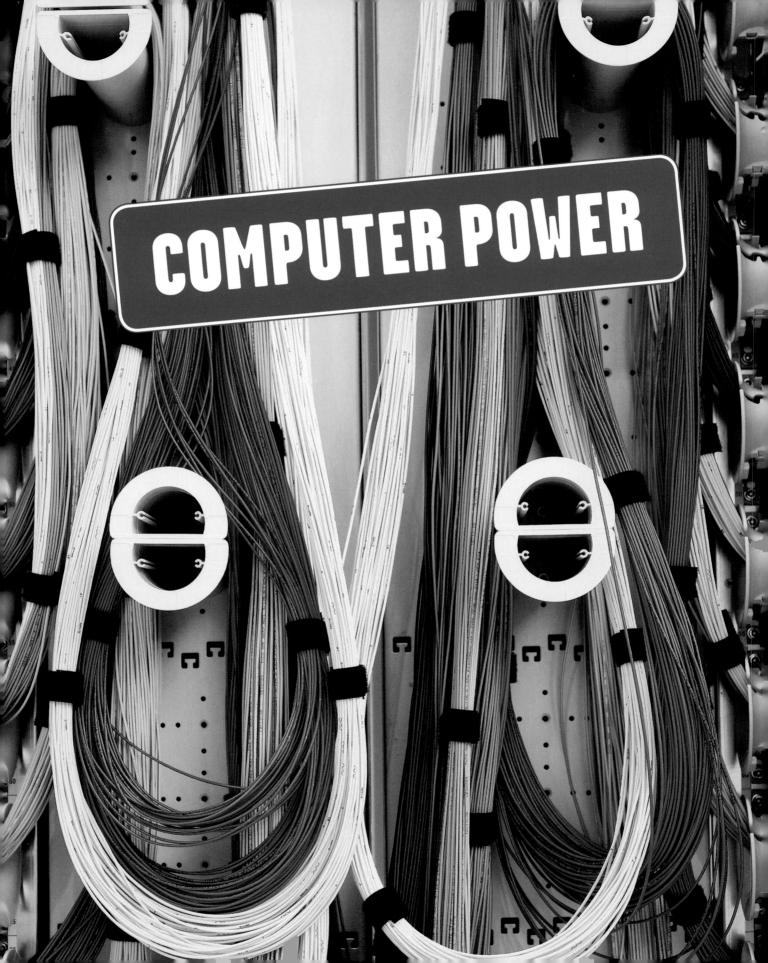

COMPUTER POWER

MOSSAD SPIES ARE SMART.

They hack into computers. Then
they can see hidden files.

SPYING IS A RISKY JOB.

Eli Cohen worked undercover. He
moved to Syria in 1962. He seemed
like a rich businessman. But he
was a spy for Israel!

AFTER THEY FINISH ONE JOB,

spies get a new one. They usually get a new **disguise**, too. Mossad spies do whatever it takes to keep Israel safe.

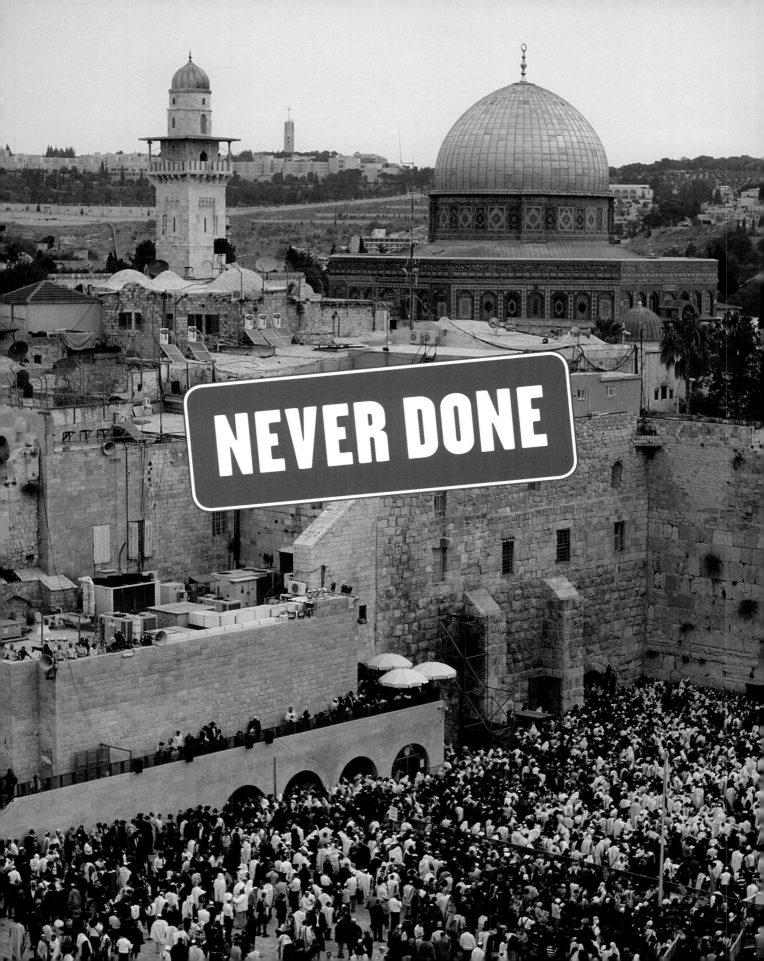

TOP-SECRET ACTIVITY

#5210: Track a Spy

A spy travels around the world. Pretend you are a spy, and write a story about your life as a secret agent!

Tools:

world map or globe
paper
crayons, markers, or
    other art supplies

Orders: Look at a world map or globe, and choose a country. If you were a spy there, what would your name be? What language would you speak? What skills would you need? Draw a picture of your disguise!

Why is it important for spies to know about other countries?

GLOSSARY

agents   people who work as spies

disguise   a change in how someone looks

hack   to use a computer to break into another system

Nazi   a member of a group in Germany that did not like Jews

tailing   following in secret

undercover   working in secret and pretending to be someone else

READ MORE

Stewart, James. *Spies and Traitors.* North Mankato, Minn.: Smart Apple Media, 2008.

Walker, Kate, and Elaine Argaet. *So You Want to Be a Spy.* North Mankato, Minn.: Smart Apple Media, 2004.

WEBSITES

THE FUR, FIN, AND FEATHER BUREAU OF INVESTIGATION
http://www.fffbi.com/
Test your spy skills with training games and quizzes.

INTERNATIONAL SPY MUSEUM: KIDSPY ZONE
http://www.spymuseum.org /education-programs/kids -families/kidspy-zone/
Play spy games, and learn how to talk like a secret agent.

Note: Every effort has been made to ensure that the websites listed above are suitable for children, that they have educational value, and that they contain no inappropriate material. However, because of the nature of the Internet, it is impossible to guarantee that these sites will remain active indefinitely or that their contents will not be altered.

INDEX